W. A. MOZART

T0195297

FLUTE CONCERTO NO. 1 IN G MAJOR, K. 313

PLAYBACK+

Speed • Pitch • Balance • Loop

To access audio visit:
www.halleonard.com/mylibrary

Enter Code
7153-4102-8266-6884

ISBN 978-1-59615-277-9

mmo Music Minus One

EXCLUSIVELY DISTRIBUTED BY

Hal•Leonard®

© 2008 MMO Music Group, Inc.
All Rights Reserved

For all works contained herein:
Unauthorized copying, arranging, adapting, recording, Internet posting, public performance,
or other distribution of the music in this publication is an infringement of copyright.
Infringers are liable under the law.

Visit Hal Leonard Online at
www.halleonard.com

Contact us:
Hal Leonard
7777 West Bluemound Road
Milwaukee, WI 53213
Email: info@halleonard.com

In Europe, contact:
Hal Leonard Europe Limited
42 Wigmore Street
Marylebone, London, W1U 2RN
Email: info@halleonardeurope.com

In Australia, contact:
Hal Leonard Australia Pty. Ltd.
4 Lentara Court
Cheltenham, Victoria, 3192 Australia
Email: info@halleonard.com.au

MOZART: Concerto In G Major, K.313

4 taps signal re-entry of orchestra.

* Because there is no orchestral accompaniment during the cadenza between measures 211 and 235, the accompaniment track of this movement is split. When performing with the accompaniment track, have a friend begin playing "Orchestra re-entry" at measure 235.

6

* Because there is no orchestral accompaniment during the cadenza, the accompaniment track of this movement is split. When performing with the accompaniment track, have a friend begin playing "Orchestra re-entry" during this trill. There will be 8 taps during the trill before the orchestra enters with the soloist's D.

8

Rondo
Tempo di Menuetto

* Because there is no orchestral accompaniment during the cadenza, the accompaniment track of this movement is split. When performing with the accompaniment track, have a friend begin playing "Orchestra re-entry" at during the held low D. There will be 3 taps before the orchestra enters with the soloist's D quarter notes.

MORE GREAT FLUTE PUBLICATIONS FROM
Music Minus One

CLASSICAL BY COMPOSER

J.S. Bach – Sonata No. 1 in B Minor; Kuhlau – Two Duets
00400360 Book/2-CD Pack......................$19.99

J.S. Bach – Suite No. 2 for Flute & Orchestra in B Minor, BWV1067
00400335 Book/Online Audio $16.99

Handel – Six Sonatas for Flute & Piano
00400377 Book/Online Audio $16.99

Handel, Telemann & Marcello – 3 Flute Sonatas
00400366 Book/Online Audio $16.99

Haydn – Flute Concerto; Vivaldi – Bullfinch Concerto; Frederick "The Great" – Flute Concerto
00400337 Book/CD Pack...........................$19.99

Mozart – Concerto No. 1 in G Major, K313
00400050 Book/Online Audio $19.99

Mozart – Concerto for Flute & Harp in C Major, KV299
00400110 Book/Online Audio $19.99

Mozart – Flute Concerto No. 2 in D Major, K. 314; Quantz – Flute Concerto in G Major
00400057 Book/Online Audio $22.99

Mozart – Quartet in F Major, KV370; Stamitz – Quartet in F Major, Op. 8 No. 3
00400341 Book/CD Pack...........................$14.99

Quantz – Trio Sonata in C Minor; J.S. Bach – Gigue from Sonata No. 1 in C Major; Abel – Sonata No. 2 in F Major
00400363 Book/CD Pack...........................$14.99

Reinecke – Concerto and Ballade for Flute & Orchestra
00400673 Book/Online Audio $22.99

Telemann – Concerto No. 1 in D Major; Corrette – Sonata in E Minor
00400364 Book/CD Pack...........................$14.99

Vivaldi – Flute Concerti in D Major, RV429; G Major, RV435; A Minor RV440
00400348 Book/Online Audio................$14.99

Vivaldi – The Four Seasons for Flute
00400672 Book/Online Audio $22.99

Vivaldi – Three Concerti for Flute & Orchestra
00400347 Book/Online Audio $22.99

Vivaldi, Bosmortier & Telemann – Three Trio Sonatas for Flute or Violin
00400378 Book/Online Audio $16.99

OTHER FLUTE COLLECTIONS

Classic Rags for Flute & Piano
00400060 Book/CD Pack...........................$14.99

The Joy of Woodwind Music
00400354 Book/CD Pack $14.99

17 Jazz Duets for Two Flutes
00400117 Book/CD Pack $14.99

Gary Shocker – Flute Duets with Piano
00400700 Book/Online Audio..............$24.99

Gary Shocker – Flute Pieces with Piano
00400699 Book/4-CD Pack $19.99

Southern Winds: Jazz Flute Jam
00400135 Book/CD Pack...........................$14.99

Three Sonatas for Flute
00400365 Book/CD Pack...........................$14.99

EASY/BEGINNING LEVEL

Easy Flute Solos
00400350 Book/2-CD Pack......................$19.99

Flute Songs – Easy Familiar Classics with Orchestra
00400346 Book/Online Audio................$19.99

World Favorites – Beginning Level
00400369 Book/CD Pack...........................$14.99

Prices, contents and availability subject to change without notice.

INTERMEDIATE LEVEL

Classic Themes from Great Composers (Intermediate)
00400370 Book/Online Audio................$16.99

Intermediate Flute Solos
00400132 Volume 2/CD............................$14.99
00400576 Volume 3/Online Audio $16.99
00400580 Volume 4/CD............................$14.99

ADVANCED LEVEL

Advanced Flute Solos
00400133 Volume 1/Online Audio.........$16.99
00400352 Volume 2/Online Audio $16.99
00400587 Volume 3/CD $14.99
00400588 Volume 5/Online Audio......$16.99

FLUTE/GUITAR DUETS

Bossa, Samba and Tango Duets for Flute & Guitar
00400134 Book/Online Audio................$19.99

Castelnuovo-Tedesco – Sonatina for Flute & Guitar, Op. 205; Guiliani – Serenata, Op. 127
00400591 Book/2-CD Pack......................$19.99

Flute & Guitar Duets
00400051 Volume 1/Online Audio........$19.99
00400144 Volume 2/Online Audio.......$19.99

Piazzolla: Histoire du Tango and Other Latin Classics
00400058 Book/Online Audio...............$24.99

HAL•LEONARD®

For songlists, to see a full listing of Music Minus One publications, or to order from your favorite music retailer, visit

halleonard.com/ MusicMinusOne

0122
242